Seven Paths to Happiness
(*and two dead ends*)

Seven Paths to Happiness

(and two dead ends)

Strategies for your life and career

Chris Croft

First published in the UK in 2024

Book design: Adam Hay Studio, UK

Paperback
ISBN: 9798878993623

Introduction

There isn't one best way to live your life...

... because our personalities and our situations vary. But there are different options that can work. And certainly there are bad ways which result in dead ends, and good ways that have risks. Maybe it's worth doing a bit of planning ahead as one's life unfolds, rather than following the turnings and choices at random. A map of the maze might make it less fun, but would be useful. Although maybe just to explore the maze at random is one of the options??

I've been thinking about this for 30 years now and I would like to propose seven options for how you could live your life successfully. I've seen people doing all seven of these (in fact I have lurched between several of them myself) and some people have done them well and some badly. Some have taken one or other of the dead ends and it hasn't ended well for them. And since we only get one life it's worth trying to do the best we can with the one chance we get.

Kierkegaard said "Life is lived forwards but can only be understood backwards" but I don't entirely agree with this – we can make better decisions as we come to key moments if we learn from our path so far, and have an understanding of where our happiness comes from, where success comes from, and whether we want one or both – and in what ratio. Maximising the effectiveness of your chosen life path would mean maximising the happiness and success that your path delivers, not just at the end but, more importantly, during the journey.

So the questions are

- What are the possible paths?
- Which one are you already on?
- Are you happy with the one you're on?
- Which path would be best for you?
- Can you change path?
- How can you maximise the effectiveness of your chosen path?

Big questions indeed, but I've got some great answers for you.

So let's dive in!

Contents

The Meaning of Life

Happiness and success, enjoy and achieve

Before we get onto the seven paths to a successful or happy life we need to think about what IS a "successful" or a "happy" or a "good" life?

I would like to suggest that the answer is to maximise both your enjoyment and your achievement – happiness and success.

Enjoyment in the present
Achievement in the future.

Are these inter-related? Yes! Too much of one means you might miss out on the other. But also, a decent amount of one leads to MORE of the other.

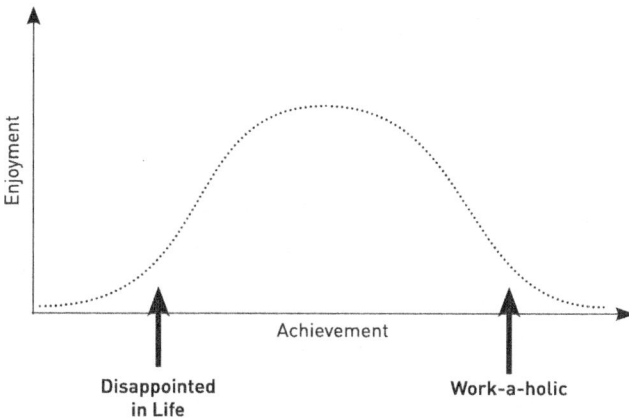

Or, seen from the other angle:

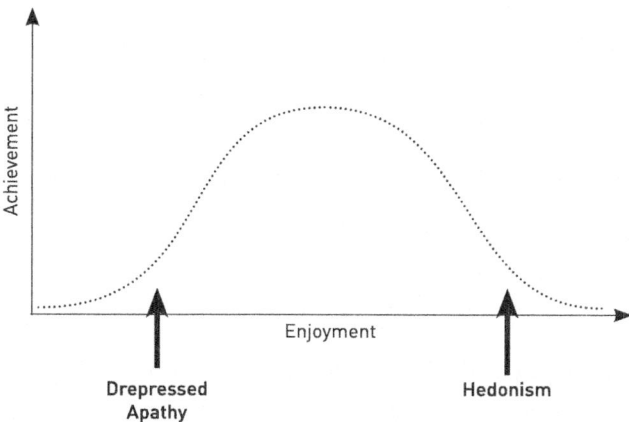

So if you're doing something that you enjoy you're more likely to be successful at it (it's very hard to be successful at something you don't enjoy). And if you're getting some success at what you're doing that's going to give you more enjoyment as well. Can a person enjoy something when they're NOT being successful? Yes, but with difficulty!

But if you focus completely on enjoyment then you become less likely to be successful since there has to be SOME work, some moments where you have to be disciplined and do some things you don't feel like doing today, in order to be successful tomorrow.

Similarly, if you focus completely on success then you may not have the time or opportunity to have fun.

What comes first, happiness or success?

There is the possible choice of having fun first and then getting around to success later, or being successful at all costs and then (when rich?) having the fun you have waited for. We'll come to these ideas later but you can probably already see the snags with both of these plans…

So a certain amount of enjoyment and achievement is best – whether they are 70/30, 50/50 or 30/70 is yet to be decided, but not 100-0 or 0-100 for sure, and probably not 90/10.

Home vs Work

One more ingredient to this is the split of time and energy between Home and Work.

Some people have the plan:

- Minimum effort at work
- Maximum enjoyment at home (as in "outside work")

This isn't a good plan. We'll come back to that shortly.
A better plan, which many would subscribe to, is

- Maximum achievement at work
- Maximum enjoyment at home (by which I mean everything outside of your work)

But that's still missing out on 50% of both the fun and success that you could have!

How about:

- Maximum achievement AND enjoyment at work

- Maximum enjoyment AND achievement at home

Is this possible?   Yes, for sure!

We've already seen how achievement leads to more enjoyment, and enjoyment leads to more achievement, so why not try to do as much of all of them as you can, in all places?

Happiness = Enjoyment + Achievement

The only other assumption in all this is that happiness is a combination of having fun in the present and then achieving as much as possible in the future (or, when you get there, in the present, from past efforts).

This is probably correct because there are known to be two types of happiness: Hedonistic (having fun in the now but maybe paying a price later) and Eudemonic (the feeling of life satisfaction from having achieved things in the past, so you pay a price initially and get the payback later). In the ideal life we would harvest as much as we can of both of these, in some sort of ratio: whether they are 70/30, 50/50 or 30/70 is yet to be decided, but not 100-0 or 0-100 for sure.

The options – the combinations of happiness and success

We know that an obsession with success probably leads to very little happiness, and that prioritising short term happiness probably leads to very little success. But what combinations of both are available to us?

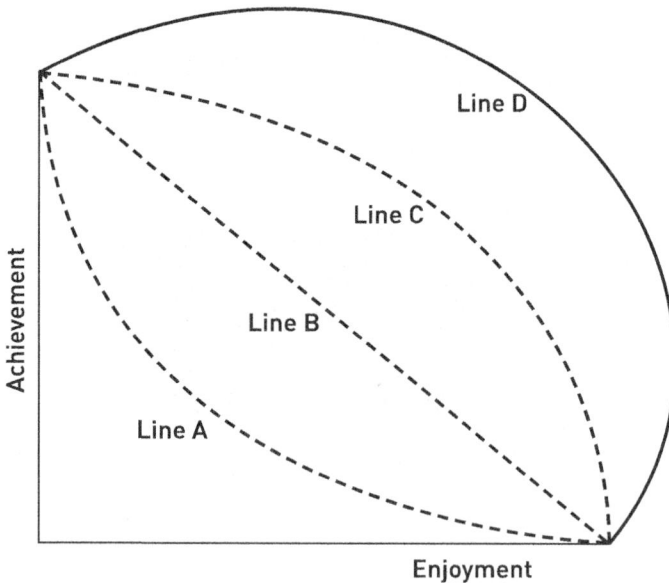

Line A would be the case if there was a conflict between achievement and enjoyment – if you had to choose mainly one or the other. For example if you go for medium achievement you get quite low enjoyment. Some people believe this is how the world works, but I don't.

Line B would be the zero-sum line – if you gain on one you lose the same amount on the other. Every bit of achievement you gain means a corresponding loss of enjoyment. Every gain in enjoyment means you have to give up the same amount of achievement.

Line C would be a world where they enhance each other – if you have a bit of each you will be doing better than you would be by focusing on just one or the other. You only have to pay a small price in happiness if you want to increase your achievement quite a bit, and you can get a large increase in happiness for only a small sacrifice of achievement.

Line D is where there is positive synergy between Achievement and Enjoyment. By achieving a little bit you can enjoy yourself more than if you ignored achievement and focussed only on enjoying yourself. And by enjoying yourself a little bit you can achieve more than you could if you ignored enjoyment and focussed on 100% achievement. But there is still a point where increasing your achievement will reduce your happiness, and a point where increasing your happiness does mean you have to achieve less.

I believe **line D** is how the world works.

Important: not everybody is ON this line! In fact very few people are, because this is the optimal line, the maximum combination of achievement and enjoyment we can achieve. Most of us are somewhere in the space UNDER line D. Some are not achieving much, for various reasons, maybe they haven't yet found the right job. Others are not very happy, for many other reasons.

Our objective is to get to the line, and in fact, to be on the best point on the line.

Where is that "best" point?

It's very hard
to be successful
at something you
don't enjoy

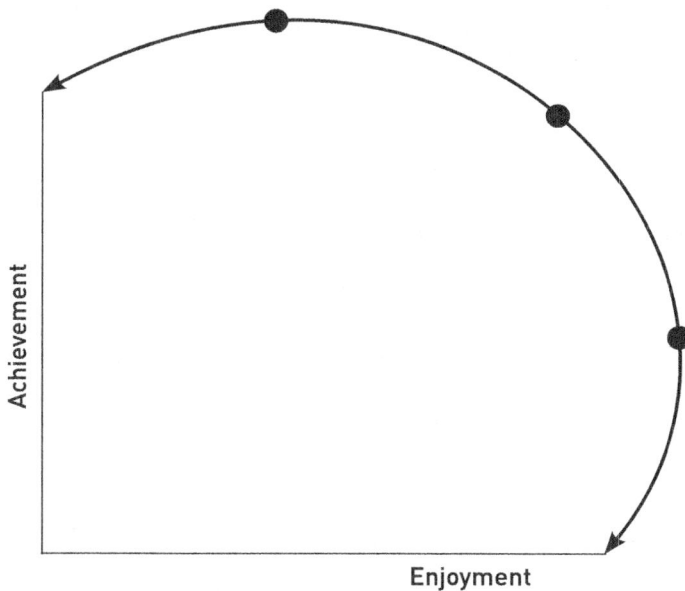

You could be an achievement maximiser, or get quite a bit of both, or you could be an enjoyment maximiser.

But if you add the two together you get some sort of measure of total happiness in life, and I think the combination of a bit of both gets the best score.

Let's put some numbers to this. They are going to be quite arbitrary, just some sort of score for your perceived "achievement/happiness out of ten" but better than nothing, and maybe helpful for thinking about this tricky but incredibly important concept.

Life Happiness = Enjoyment x Achievement

With the numbers, since we instinctively want a balance of both achievement and enjoyment, I would like to suggest that life happiness is not just achievement PLUS enjoyment, it's achievement TIMES enjoyment.

If that's the case then the balanced mixture of both is by far the best target to aim for. (And incidentally the strategies of "all achievement" or "all happiness" both do really badly – as they should).

17

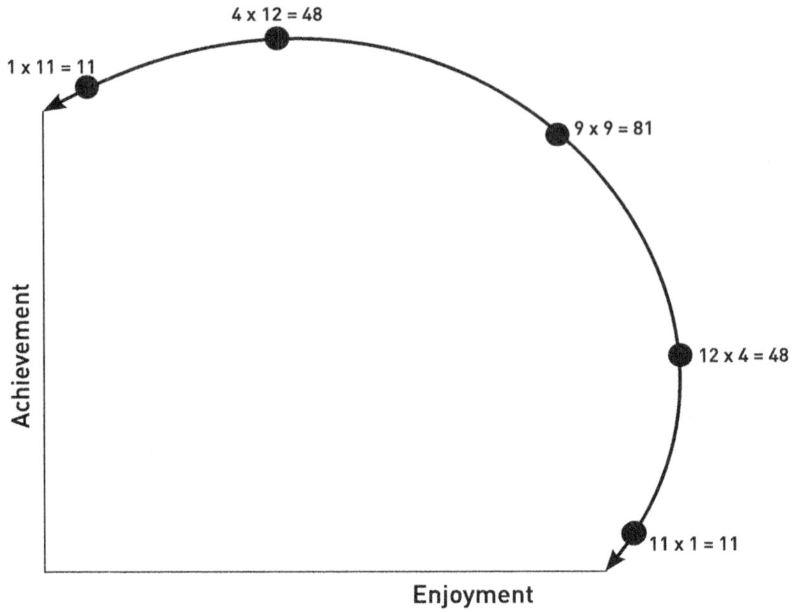
4 x 12 = 48
1 x 11 = 11
9 x 9 = 81
12 x 4 = 48
11 x 1 = 11
Achievement
Enjoyment

How to get to the ideal point, of a mixture of enjoyment and achievement in our lives?

Would it be better to start on the Achieve path and then, at a certain point, cut across horizontally towards happiness?

Or maybe have fun first and then get around to achievement later.....

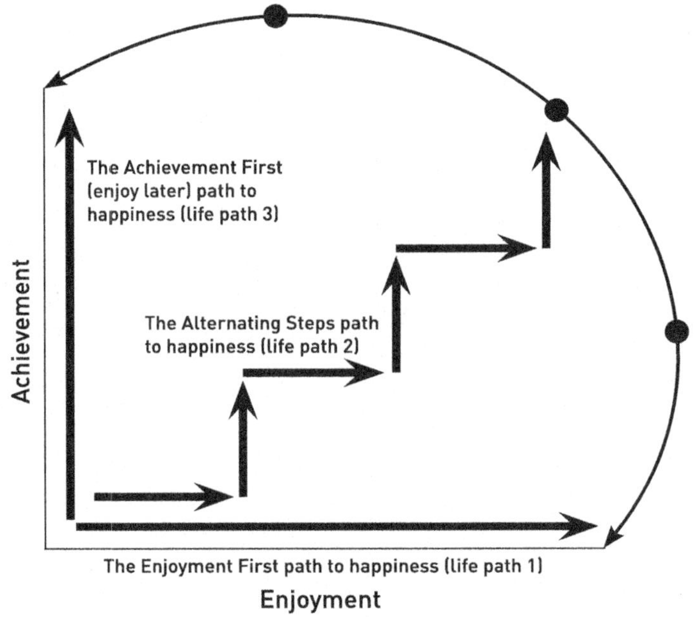
The Achievement First
(enjoy later) path to
happiness (life path 3)
The Alternating Steps path
to happiness (life path 2)
The Enjoyment First path to happiness (life path 1)
Achievement
Enjoyment

If you focus
completely on
success then you
may not have the
time or opportunity
to have fun

You could be an achievement maximiser, or you could be an enjoyment maximiser

"Enjoy now and achieve later" clearly has its risks ("jam tomorrow" which never comes) while "achieve now and enjoy later", the idea that once we've made it we can sit back and enjoy ourselves, has the risk that we never make it "enough" and we get addicted to working.

Doing both, steadily at the same time, seems to be the best way, if you can do it.

These three options are my first three Life paths: paths 1 2 and 3 – next we will have a closer look at them and then we will see the other four choices…

Introduction to the paths

I've tried to put the 7 paths in a logical order, or at least one that has a flow from each path to the next. But it is important to say that *they aren't in any order of preference.*

Is there an 8th one, that I haven't thought of? Maybe! I certainly can't prove that there isn't. But 7 is enough to be getting on with – and there is something for everyone here.

The objective is to give you food for thought rather than one right answer. Although you may well decide that one path is perfect for you, or that two or three look suitable and are worth investigating in more detail.

As we'll see later, you can do one path for your whole life, or a mixture of two or three at once, or one for half your life, or just for a few years, and then change to another.

The main thing is if you choose a path, to do it well.

And to avoid both of the dead ends!

Path 1
Maximum fun until it runs out...

Who knows what you'll learn along the way

The plan with this first possible path is to have as much fun as you can – just take the choice of activity or work that is most attractive and go for it. Say yes to everything that appeals to you. There's plenty of time later in life to settle down, get a job or learn a skill, and to achieve stuff - especially if you're in your 20s, and maybe even if you're in your 30s. (Or 40s??).

In fact if you keep your living costs down you could maybe bounce along under the radar for a long time, maybe even your whole life! Just having a good time while ambitious people pointlessly burn themselves out making money that they can't take with them when they go.

Why not??

And "till it runs out" doesn't mean until the money runs out, or until the fun runs out (providers of fun will always be there) - it means until you get bored of the fun.

Pros and cons

I think the advantage of this path is that if you don't have fun in your 20's then when WILL you have fun?? When WILL you take some risks, travel, explore, experiment, discover the world and yourself?

And who knows what you'll learn along the way – perhaps options for running your own business will come from the people you meet and the places you go.

You might even accidentally achieve some things as well; when you're enjoying doing something you quite often do it really well, so who knows where it'll lead...

And it's quite true that there's no rush – you can think about kids and pensions when you're 30, for sure. And if you find a way to keep on doing it, then you can decide whether to keep doing it when you get to 30, ...or at whatever age the choice feels more serious.

What's the downside?

Well, it could be a decade wasted. If you decide later that there's something you really want to spend your life on, you've lost ten years. And possibly the most energetic and creative part of your life, the time when it's easiest to make new contacts, learn new skills, and change direction.

Also it could become a habit – you might become that person who doesn't settle down, or doesn't focus, and never really achieves anything, which you might feel unhappy about later. You might end up short of money, short of a sense of achievement, feeling that life has slipped through your fingers somehow.

Also you still have to earn enough money to live, and if you get a job that is easy to get (e.g. waiting tables or delivery driver) or fun (music teacher or dive instructor) then it probably won't be very well paid, because lots of other people will be in the market for that job too. So you'll have to work quite a lot of hours just to survive, and you won't have much money. This may not be a problem, for example if you're living abroad somewhere cheap, but it's a factor to consider.

And finally, that hedonistic decade might not be as much fun as you think it will be. It might:

- get repetitive,

- you might miss the intellectual challenge that only work can give,

- it might feel a bit empty,

- you might feel a lack of achievement from month to month,

- ...and it might take a physical toll (depending on what you're doing – if it's, say, surfing or mountain biking them you might be in great shape, but if it's partying then you may not).

But if you CAN really enjoy your 20s and THEN take one of the other paths, that could be a great result!

Tips to maximise the success of this path

Of course you don't have to commit to a whole decade of fun before you'll get down to achieving something - you can take it year by year. Each year take a moment to review and ask yourself "Is this still REALLY great, or am I getting bored now?" and if it's still great, carry on!

And you can mix this path with others – you can have a little bit of work going on as you party, or you can be looking for your Ikigai (more on that later) as you travel the world. You could get enough feeling of success from this small amount of work, and you could already be planning a bit for the next phase while you are in this phase – as long as you don't ruin it with too much planning, too much living in the future.

So this path doesn't have to involve a decade of shallow frippery, it could be a phase of your life where you are an adventurer, discovering what you love and don't love, pushing yourself, building your skills, and making some great memories.

Feathered Transition

You don't have to *suddenly* stop the fun phase and begin the work phase. You could start a part time job, or start working on your own business one day a week, and see if it builds up or not, see how it feels.

Feathering is how pilots slowly change the shape of the wings (with flaps) to gradually change direction or height (I think).

Phase 1

Phase 2

Generally I'm a fan of feathered transitions, rather than sudden changes. For example I am retiring from training gradually, stopping working on Fridays, then Mondays as well, then dropping from 3 days to 2 days a week and then to just 4 days a month. So there's no shock in terms of suddenly having no purpose, suddenly telling my customers I'm gone, etc. And I can see how I feel as the fade-out (or fade-in of retired life) slowly happens.

Another feathered transition I would recommend is to start a side hustle slowly, in the evenings or for one day a week, and see how it goes, building it gradually – rather than resigning and going for it 100% from day 1, which is risky and stressful – and probably impossible.

When I was an Operations Manager is was a known fact that you can never get a step change in production, it always has to gradually change over to a new process or gradually ramp up. If you buy a new machine it won't work on day 1. New people don't produce much on day 1. It's just not a good plan to have a step change, for anything. Always better to feather. Anyway, more talk about how to set up your own business in later paths...

The decade (or however long) won't be wasted if:

- You have harvested a lot of happiness from it

- You have learned from it: collected some useful things for the next phase of your life. To this end I would recommend keeping a journal, not in any heavy way but just recording interesting ideas, things you could buy or sell, things you could learn or do, people you could work with, if your next phase turns out to be running your own business. Also record things you enjoy doing, things you're good at, and contacts you've made, in case you end up searching for your Ikigai (more later on that!) or just looking for your ideal job.

People who this path might suit

It's a fine line to walk – to succeed at this path you have to be good enough at enjoying yourself to really have fun, (I'm too serious, I plan ahead too much, I would struggle with it, to be honest) but you also need to be controlled enough to give up the party life at the right time. Too much partying, or not enough partying, are both risks. How much of a party animal are you?

Too much partying,
or not enough partying,
are both risks.

Dead end 1
Easy life
at work

A path that many people seem to be taking is to aim for an easy life at work, so you get maximum time and energy for your personal life – family, friends, fun stuff.

Having realised that work is never going to be fun, and that any achievement you make at work just makes your boss or the company richer and not you, then why should you bother to make an effort??

If you've chosen this path then it's not your fault, it's the fault of your organisation for not involving you, not getting your buy-in. You should feel part of where you work, not just an employee. You should be financially and emotionally rewarded for what you achieve for them. In fact it should feel as if you're achieving it for yourself, not just for the company and the customers.

But this is all too rare. You could wait a long time to find a good boss who motivated you at work, or to find an employer who incentivised you fairly.

So I would like to suggest that even if there is no apparent benefit to be gained from doing a good job, you should still work as hard as you can and do the best you can at work, because a) YOU'll know, and b) they might notice and reward you. And if they don't notice, you can leave and look for somewhere better.

I just think the life strategy of finding a job where you can do the minimum – in order to pay the wages while conserving your energy for the time outside of work - is a waste of 5 days a week for most of your life, and that's too big a chunk of time to have as 'dead'.

It's bad enough to get all your achievement and no enjoyment from work, but to get *neither* is truly a waste.

Could it ever end well?

This strategy could only be a good one if your personal life was AMAZING, say you were working on a cure for cancer or writing the next Dark Side of the Moon (yes, to me they are on a similar level) and you just had to pay the bills while you did it.

Especially if it was a temporary situation, just a year and then it's done.

What if you were building your own workshop and once it's done you can chuck in your job at the Council and start running your own business – that would be fine because your life path is the new business; the job you don't care about isn't your life path.

But we all tell ourselves things are temporary, and then ten years have got behind us, so this really MUST be temporary if you're doing it!

Small achievements

There's a difficult grey area – I have to admit I can't define where the edge is, you'll just have to think about whether it's enough for you: what if you quite enjoy your job, and you do also get a feeling of achievement from it? Not particularly that it's building up or moving forwards, just that each day you achieve stuff, and you're reasonably happy with that? *Is that enough??*

For example, say you work as a receptionist, and every day you sort out a whole lot of visitors with questions, you juggle the calls and the people at the desk, and you go home feeling good about your day of work. Is that OK? Should you be aiming higher than that?

I would say if you enjoy it and you get a feeling of achievement from it, then it's fine.

Another example could be what my friend Keith Thomson calls a Comfortable Loyalist – for example an engineer who works for the same company for years, enjoying their work, perhaps getting promoted a little bit - but that's not why they do it, they do it because the work is interesting and enjoyable, and not stressful, the company looks after them, and they have plenty of energy for their personal life as well.

They've not chosen the *lowest* path, they've chosen a comfortable path that still gives enjoyment and achievement, and I think that's great.

It's bad enough
to get all your
achievement and
no enjoyment from
work, but to get
neither is truly
a waste.

...as long as...

- You don't suddenly think "Why have I done this for so long??" and regret the lost time, or if

- There's something else you could be doing that would be MORE enjoyable and/or produce MORE achievement, and you're not looking for it / finding it because you've "settled".

If you've already started 'settling' - or doing a job you don't care about because it's easy...

There are many paths you can go by, but in the long run there's always still time to change the road you're on. While you continue your job that doesn't excite you but which you need because it pays the bills, you can start working on one or more side hustles, looking for your Ikigai, learning about a niche – all the things we will be considering in this book.

At least consider it – you don't need to do anything right now, nothing drastic anyway, just read this book and see if any of the ideas grab you as interesting, or 'better than your current path'.

Path 2

Steadily up the mountain

On this path we are going to climb a mountain of achievement, but in small steady risk-free steps, enjoying it along the way. That would be a good life!

The commonest example of this would be a classic career – working your way up the corporate ladder, either within one company or by jumping between them, until you are well paid, doing interesting work, and can really make a difference, ideally with a nice pension as well.

But it could also describe someone slowly building their own business, gradually adding customers, or products, even employees, along the way. Generally 'Lifestyle Businesses', from a trainer like me to a builder, or as property developer or financial adviser or a landscape gardener – businesses where you employ nobody or perhaps just a PA – these can be built slowly like this. A business where you employ lots of people and plan to sell it off one day would be in Path 3, coming up next. (You can't easily sell a lifestyle business because it's just you).

There are three potential problems with slowly climbing ONE BIG mountain:

- You might never quite make it to the summit (and on real mountains people would sometimes rather die than come back down having only climbed 99% of the mountain)

- If you succeed, what do you do after that? How do you follow Mount Everest? Or a gold medal? Or selling your company off? You have to either

  - find something even BIGGER (and be more likely to fail) – and it keeps escalating until eventually you DO fail,

  - or you have to keep doing the SAME AGAIN and again, endlessly, with less enjoyment each time - and a continuing risk of failing. This is what happens to some Olympic medallists.

  - Or you have to put that epic achievement behind you and do SMALLER things which will never have quite the same appeal. Imagine climbing smaller mountains after you've done Everest! Or entering local competitions after you've got an Olympic gold. What a come-down!

Enjoy the climbing, not just the arrival at the summit

- All the achievement is at the end, which will leave you feeling starved of achievement *during the process*. That's fine if the mountain only takes a few days to climb, but if it's your whole life and the achievement is right at the end, that's not a good plan.

So the idea of this path is that yes, you're going to climb a mountain, but to make it successful you are going to do two things:

- **Enjoy the climbing,** not just the arrival at the summit, since 99% of the time is spent during the climbing. And if you don't or can't enjoy the climbing, then don't do it, even if you LOVE briefly standing on summits.

- As well as enjoyment along the way, try to get a feeling of **achievement along the way** as well. So the mountain would be a series of small achievements, each ridge is an achievement where you can pause and take in the view. Maybe even sometimes reset your path at that point, now you have a better perspective. So you'll definitely have a constant feeling of achievement during your life, and what you learn during the process will help with the bigger achievements that you will create later.

Pros and cons

Even though you're doing it piecemeal, and taking stock after each step you achieve, you will need a longer-term bigger-picture plan. Which direction are you working towards?

And after you've spent a few years and made a few steps up, you are reasonably committed to this path. Yes you can change, but that will have some cost.

I realised that being an Engineer wasn't for me, and then I realised that being a Manager wasn't for me either, and both of these "false starts" cost me time: years in fact. But one could argue that the learning always comes in handy for later paths. And at least if you enjoy them (unfortunately I didn't) then you didn't waste the years from the *enjoyment* point of view, only the achievement point of view.

Also this relatively cautious process of, say, building a business in small steps, or making a difference in small steps, will be slower than going for it 100% in one big all-or-nothing surge.

Finally, some things CAN'T be done in this cautious way – for example it would be difficult to train as a nurse and then a physio and then a doctor: you have to decide on 'Doctor 'and then go for that (we'll see this path in options 3 and 4 later).

Pitfalls and how to avoid them / make them less likely

We've already seen that the biggest risk is that the steps are heading in the wrong direction, and maybe we don't realise, or don't want to admit it, until we're quite committed. The sunk cost fallacy!

So if you're starting to feel that it's not the best way for you after all, then it's important to stop and have a re-think. You've got more time in your life than you think! I know people who have started new careers at 50 and even 60. Better to do that than to keep ploughing on when you're not happy.

There's also a risk that this path focusses too much on achievement and so enjoyment gets forgotten. Taking time to savour the view as you go up the mountain needs some effort to "be present", and similarly as you build up skills or move to different jobs or gain bigger contracts it's important to stand back and get some enjoyment as well.

The corporate career might never be fun or satisfying, you might never be able to make a difference, you might never reach that high level you aspire to.

There's also the work/life balance element: it's easy and tempting to let the excitement of your work success squeeze out time spent on your personal and social life.

And finally there's the question of when to stop, if ever. When you get to a certain level of achievement, where you're still comfortable but feeling good, is it OK to stop? Do you continue until you reach your level of incompetence, where you'll be less happy (and also feel bad about going back) or do you stop and always wonder whether going a bit higher would have been even better?

Be yourself as much as you can, unless you're pretty sure it's going to upset someone – but then, why would it?

I don't think it's possible to answer this last point, I think you just have to weigh it up when you get there. Just don't get addicted to moving on up, if it's not making you happier. It might be better to add a new second staircase, which we'll consider later when we get to the idea of multi-harvesting.

Maximise the chance of succeeding in corporate life

In the case of having the best journey up the corporate ladder, I would suggest the following points:

- Be T-shaped, so you know a bit about a lot of things (e.g. both engineering and sales) and a lot about something – be the authority, the expert on something (e.g. India, or Pay Per Click, or the machining of gear wheels)

- Be very easy to deal with – always the same, always reliable, always on time, always delivering work by the promised date, always getting back to people when they leave you a message, always positive and polite.

- Always be smart, ready to see an important customer if needed

- No enemies, be the friend of everyone. Make the effort to get to know everyone, be a great listener.

- Volunteer for projects, be the one to volunteer to do the talk at the conference in Australia – who knows where that might lead! And learn about presentation skills so you are ready if asked.

- Learn as much as you can about everything, go on every course you can, learn about negotiating and selling, leadership, marketing and strategy, etc

- Be yourself as much as you can, unless you're pretty sure it's going to upset someone – but then, why would it?

- Help others whenever you can – this is great for learning, for building up goodwill, and for your happiness!

- Know what your next step on the ladder is going to be. For example if the next step is to work in the USA, make sure you visit there and meet as many colleagues as you can there, learn all about the USA operation, so you're clearly ready, you're the obvious candidate. If your next step is to move from Technical to Marketing, then go on a course, work on some joint projects, make sure you have the skills (or at least some of them) and have shown an interest, BEFORE the job comes up.

Backup plans

In the corporate world this means keeping your CV ready, keeping an eye on the job market, making and keeping plenty of contacts in other companies, so that if you have to move then you can. Sometimes your face just doesn't fit, or something changes (e.g. the company who employs you is bought by another larger one) and it's time to move on.

Jam tomorrow

Another risk with the corporate ladder plan is the situation where your career just doesn't really go anywhere, or the promotions are really slow, and you end up repeatedly thinking "I'll just give it one more year" – at what point do you knock it on the head, maybe decide to leave and work somewhere else, or try a completely different life plan? All I can say is keep questioning it, maybe ask a trusted friend whether it's time to vote with your feet, and then do what they say. It'll be obvious to an outsider, but not to you! Have the guts to move if your plan isn't working out.

Switching between companies

My simplified diagram of going up the staircase of success could in real life look a lot more messy (and risky!).

You might move to a job where the promises never materialise and the planned promotions don't happen.

You might have to take a short term demotion to get onto a better ladder, or you might make an immediate jump (as shown here):

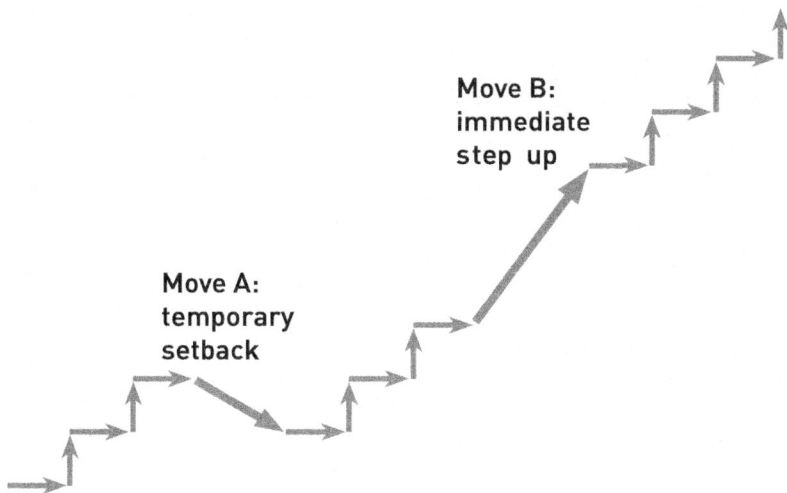

Move B:
immediate
step up

Move A:
temporary
setback

People who this path might suit

Maybe you want to achieve something or reach a particular level – perhaps you already know what it is, perhaps you don't, but you know there is something out there for you and that upwards is your direction of travel – but you don't want to take a big risk and commit 100% to a big goal all in one go.

If you're good at playing the political game, of getting along with everyone and making sure your face fits, and good at presenting your views to key people in key moments - then you'll do well at this path.

If you're patient, and more importantly good at enjoying each step along the way, then this could work well for you.

If you're the kind of person who would rather work steadily on something, one step at a time, adapting your plan as you go, then this could be the path for you.

Path 3

One big plan, with delayed gratification

This path could be your whole life or just part of it, maybe with something else before it or something else after it. The path involves working on something big, with complete commitment. It is mainly concerned with success, and then the plan is to get *some* happiness during the build and *a lot* of happiness once the build is done.

Usually this path is for someone who is building their own company – where you create an organisation with yourself at the top of it, with the intention of selling it at some point. At this point someone else will have to run it, so you'll need to go from being the all knowing essential creator to someone who has set up systems and trained up people so that you can sneak off sideways, take a big payment, and nobody will notice. That's the theory anyway!

Pros and cons

The advantage of this path is that you get to build something significant and great. And there's a chance - not 100% - that you'll end up with quite a bit of money afterwards (and also some power during the building, if that's what you want).

Pitfalls and how to avoid them / make them less likely

The big risk is that you won't have much fun – or any! – until you've arrived at the top. Until you've built your own company. The early years might have a lot of hard work and stress. It'll be "Jam Tomorrow" for quite a while. And of course the other HUGE risk is that it never arrives.

Building your own company is definitely difficult – it requires knowledge of buying, selling, management, finance, marketing, quality etc etc as well as determination, risk-taking, probably long hours, etc.

And then selling it off is even harder – when it's profitable you don't want to sell it, when it's not profitable you CAN'T sell it. You'll never sell it at exactly the right time. Some people never sell it, they work till they die (sometimes claiming that they love it) – or they sell it off and then die shortly afterwards, perhaps because they feel they've lost their purpose.

Are you sure you won't do this??

That's why the previous path - taking small steady steps – is easier and less risky. But this one is the only way to make a LOT of money, or to build something really significant and great.

Tips to maximise the success of this path

The two textbook responses to risk are to make it less likely and make it less serious – so you'd make sure you do everything you can to make sure you succeed, and also have a back up plan in case you don't.

Also, get as much information as you can before committing to building your life:

- What are the potential and likely problems?

- What skills and resources will you need?

- Who do you know who has done it, and what would they advise?

- (would they do it again knowing what they now know?),

- Who can you find to help you?

- What's your plan if it doesn't work?

- Can you test it in some way first?

- Or at least is there an easy bail out point not too far in?

Maximise the chance of succeeding in running your own business

In the case of building your own business there is A LOT to know! I'd read lots of books, and maybe get an MBA, but meanwhile, a few thoughts are:

- Ansoff's Matrix – make sure you explore selling all of your products (or services) to all of your existing customers, then think about which new markets there are for the products, what new things you can sell to your existing customers, and avoid new products and new markets at the same time.

- Put your prices up! People never charge as much as they should. You should be losing half of your potential business on price, otherwise you're not charging enough. If nearly everyone pays the price you ask then you are leaving money on the table – they would have paid more! At least do some experimenting.

- Start with subcontractors and leave employing full time people until you really are sure that you need them. Getting rid of them again is not easy!

- Delegate as much as you can – I know they won't do it as well as you, but you can't do everything! This allows you to free up your brain for creativity, which is your main asset.

- Never be dependent on just one employee or just one supplier, or just one customer. Too risky!

- Examine your competitors – and consider working with them in areas where you don't compete.

- Have a very clear marketing message – what do you do and what value does it add? People need to understand that in 3 seconds from your website.

- Keep an eye on response times and lead times – you might need to pay for some extra resources to keep these times down – but customer service is vitally important and often forgotten.

- Think about your exit plan as you build your business, not suddenly at the end!

Building your own company is definitely difficult - and then selling it off is even harder

Back up plans

In the case of building your own company, your back-up plan if it doesn't grow enough to be sold off is that at least you can earn a decent living from it, while staying within it. Even if it's small, even if it depends on you being part of it, at least you can earn a living from it – and nobody can fire you!

I would definitely not recommend having several businesses, or some sort of side hustle going on, because that will just dilute your effort. When I was building up my own training company I still did some training as just myself, to keep another income stream coming in, and what gradually happened was that my own training grew and grew (with lovely instant money) while the new company – which wasn't paying much yet – became neglected and never reached the level it could have.

So all your time and focus is on your one company that you are building, and if it fails, then you'll have to start something different, …or get a job. But you'll be pretty much unemployable after having been self employed I can tell you – you'll find it horrible to go back to having a boss! So you'll need to think about what to do next.

Don't think about this until you have to though – there should be no distractions while you're building your business.

More dangerous really is the case where your business just doesn't really go anywhere and you end up repeatedly thinking "I'll just give it one more year" – at what point do you knock it on the head, maybe sell it off for a small amount, and decide to try something else? All I can say is ask a trusted friend whether it's time to throw in the towel, and then do what they say. It'll be obvious to an outsider, but not to you! It's your baby! And google The Sunk Cost Fallacy one more time!

Delayed gratification working for someone else

Occasionally there are cases where you might have to go through some pain in order to get a job you really want – maybe an apprenticeship, or being a junior doctor, or get training and experience before you can work abroad or on an oil rig - or even in outer space!

These are often vocations, which will be covered next.

But in any situation like this, the same principles apply as with building your own business

- Are you sure it really will pay off later?

- Are you sure that you'll definitely enjoy the payoff when it comes?

- Will the payoff, if it comes and you enjoy it, more than compensate for the price you have had to pay?

- Since there is risk in both the above, are you happy to take that risk, and are there ways you can reduce the risk?

- If you don't enjoy the process of getting there then you are less likely to enjoy it when you do get there.

- Achievement does always require sacrifice, so I'm not against you paying a price up front – just be careful that it will be worth it, particularly when it involves employers, who often promise the earth.

- My own experience was that I had a vague feeling that being a Director would be great, but that I had to do a few years as a foot soldier (junior manager) first. It turned out that being a foot soldier was worse than I thought, and when I finally reached Director is was pretty much the same as being a foot soldier, in some ways worse: for example more stressful and more detached from the direct work and feeling of getting results. I should have investigated the price and the expected payoff more closely before setting out on that 15 year journey!

At least with building your own business you're not reliant on promises from an organisation, and the final destination is 100% owned by you.

If you don't enjoy
the process of getting
there then you are
less likely to enjoy
it when you do
get there

People who this path might suit

This is a hard path to take! You need to be tough, and flexible – to build your own business you'll need to be knowledgeable in all areas of business, able to cope with people and numbers, money and technical stuff.

You'll need to handle stress, carrying the load of the whole business on just your shoulders – possibly borrowing money, remortgaging your house, and paying yourself almost nothing during lean years.

And be ready for the long haul – it's going to take 10, maybe 20 or 30 years to do this.

But if you want to achieve something big during an exciting life, and end up with a lot of money, (hopefully to use during a long retirement) then this could be the path for you!

Dead end 2
Starting with the money

Whether you're choosing a job, or considering a side hustle, or planning a full-on self-employed business, it's tempting to think about how to make money first, rather than starting with what you are interested in or enjoy doing and letting the money sort itself out as a secondary issue.

> "How can I get rich?"
> "How can I earn enough to.....?"
> "How can I get as much money as that person over there?"

It's so easy to start with the money.

Why you might be tempted

Everything around us is shouting at us to spend money – that's what advertising does. Social media has now joined in with that. We can't help believing that money will make us happy.

Success leading to money leading to happiness

That's what we are being sold, all the time.

Why it's a bad idea

There are two problems with this though:

- If you start by thinking about the money, you won't succeed in making it – it won't work.

- If it DID work, it wouldn't make you happy anyway.

Let's just check that both of those big statements are true!

Starting with the money doesn't work

To be successful your heart has to be in it. You'll need to be creative, to care, to make sure the details are right, to go the extra mile, to put in the hours – and this just won't happen if you're only in it for the money.

Unless you enjoy
earning money because
you're doing something
you love, the price will
outweigh the gain

Starting with things you love, and things that you are already good at, HAS to be more sensible. We'll cover this more later in path 7: Searching for your Ikigai.

If there are things which you enjoy or which you are good at, but you then calculate that they aren't going to make you a living, you can ditch those ideas and think of others. But that's the order: ideas first, assess for profit: second.

Success (and therefore money) also requires you to help other people, to give them something they want or need, so again it's better to start with "What do people want?" or "What can I do for people?" rather than "How can I make money out of them?"

Money won't make you happy anyway

Suppose you could make money from some business that you didn't really care about – and some people do. Why won't it make you happy? You could buy those lovely things, maybe it would be a car, or clothes, watches, jewellery, a bigger house or a house abroad, (hey why not both??) or a horse, or expensive wine. Surely these would make you happy??

And the answer is yes, for a bit before you get bored with them (this is known as the hedonic treadmill) and they just become the accepted normal basis of your life, and then you need the NEXT step up. How quickly you get used to your new car. How quickly you want the latest sunglasses – and there's a tiny scratch on your current ones!

And yes, they do make you 10% happier – but you pay a price of 20% to earn the money. Earning money always comes with a price, and unless you enjoy earning it because you're doing something you love, the price will outweigh the gain. The long hours, the travel, the stress, the horrible boss, the scary customers, the selling of your soul – there's always at least 20% you have to pay.

Why? Because otherwise lots of other people would be doing it too, but most people have decided it's not worth the price. That senior job with the big salary – they HAVE to offer that much money to persuade good people to do that job, the job is THAT unpleasant. If it was well paid and FUN

then everyone would be queueing up to do it, and they could reduce the amount they pay.

So it's a law of nature, the price you pay will cancel out the increase in happiness - unless you LOVE what you do.

If you've already started on this...

It's never too late to change! It's hard to live on less money that you've become accustomed to, but you can gradually evolve the way you earn the money, towards doing things that are better for your soul.

Path 4
Vocation

Are you sure
you're not just
doing what one of
your parents did?

Many jobs are regarded as vocational – doctors, nurses, teachers, engineers, musicians, poets, writers, firefighters, the police, priests and preachers, joining the army maybe – we don't choose to do these jobs because of the money or the power or the security, we are drawn to them, they aren't just what we do, they are what we ARE. It was always our destiny, from a young age.

Vocations are hard to define - you could join the army or become a doctor for many different reasons, and just one of them could be that it's your vocation. Could being an accountant or an entrepreneur or a sales person be a vocation? I think so – you might be drawn to it because it's in your genes, in just the same way as medicine or fighting fires. So anything could be a vocation.

The dictionary talks about a skill or trade that you can earn your living with, like a plumber, but I think that misses the element of destiny, or being in your soul – so for example I think plumbing is a well paid and secure job, a great career choice actually, but unlikely to be in your soul. Also, if you do define vocations as "skills or trades" then accountancy and selling are skills/trades too, really – in which case almost anything could be a vocation.

Another definition of a vocation (that I like) is that it involves being of service, and maybe something you would still do even if you weren't paid for it at all (or if the pay was really bad). One could argue that teachers do it regardless of the pay being low, and musicians are also resigned to poor pay, so this definition works for them, but is being a *musician* (or any artist) really a service, in the way that a doctor or nurse or firefighter is? I know you can argue that anything that has a customer is a service (and musicians certainly do make me happy) but then accountants and lawyers surely come before musicians in that respect.... And how many doctors would do it if the pay was really bad? I'm not sure!

But whatever a vocation is, I've always been jealous of people who have one! I spent my teenage years wondering what on earth to do – as my friends slipped into being doctors or pilots I was thinking "Vet? No. Join the Navy like my dad? No. Teacher? No. Well, Engineering would keep my options open and I can do it quite well, so I'll do that for now...". I felt like a failure really because I hadn't worked out what I was, and many of my

friends had. How wonderful to know what you were born to do, and then be doing it. Clearly this is a great life path, if you're lucky enough to have been granted it.

Or is it....?

Pros and cons

Two snags with a vocation – first, how do you KNOW it's your vocation? Are you sure you're not just doing what one of your parents did, or what someone told you to do when you were younger? Doctors are often sons or daughters of doctors, engineers are often children of engineers, teachers the same, because they see the job from an early age, they know what it is and how to get into it, they are encouraged and probably helped into it by their parents – ...but is it right for them??

The second snag, and this is as big one, is that vocations may not be fun, or satisfying, or well paid. Being a doctor is going to be well paid, but not always fun or satisfying (talk to any GP or orthopaedic surgeon!), nursing isn't well paid and often isn't exactly fun, and being a musician is unlikely to be well paid. But people are drawn to these professions for whatever reason. Do they regret their choices later? I know that a lot of doctors do – I don't have statistics about teachers, though they don't seem a happy bunch. Similarly I'd love to know about musicians and poets. Causation is hard to establish too – for example, do poets get depressed or do depressives write poetry??

But still, a vocation isn't necessarily a recipe for happiness or wealth, so

- *should* we envy them if we don't have one??

- perhaps if we do have a vocational life choice we should question it? We could at least consider the idea that other paths ARE available.

... if you're lucky
you get to design
the back wheel.

Pitfalls and how to avoid them / make them less likely

To avoid choosing a vocation that won't make you happy:

- Be very careful about doing the same thing as your mother or father

- Try some other things as well as your vocation – ask yourself what would you do if you COULDN'T do your vocation

- Find out what it's REALLY like by doing some work experience early on

- Find out what it's REALLY like by talking to people who have been doing it for a long time:

- I was shocked to discover that vets don't spend the time saving the lives of animals, they mostly give out ointment, and put dogs down.

- I was also disappointed to discover that engineers don't design whole helicopters, they are one of a team of 300 who work on a new helicopter for 10 years – if you're lucky you get to design the back wheel.

- I was depressed to discover that GPs only have 6 minutes per patient, so there's no time to develop a relationship – and many of their patients are time wasters with nothing significant wrong with them.

- I was shocked to discover that orthopods do six knee operations a day; it's like a butcher hacking meat – of course they have amazing skill and we are eternally grateful to them, but to them it's a production line that they don't even see as people. Is that what you want to do for your life?

(Note, the above is slightly exaggerated for effect, but not much. No offence intended to any of these valuable professions – but every job has its pros and cons!).

Time allocation

There's one other pitfall that's particularly likely if you're pursuing a vocational life path, and that's that it takes over your life. Doctors or teachers can end up working 7 days a week, "because after all their job is much more than a job, it's what they ARE, and it's changing/saving people's lives". This is fine, if you love it and it makes you happy, but the risk is that family and friends get squeezed out, and maybe fun does too. And since your work is a never-ending stream of need, and you're really just a drop in the ocean of sick people or kids or burning houses to save, or wars to fight, are you achieving enough to give up 100% of your life to it?

So I think if you choose this path it's important to keep it under control, timewise, and make time for the other parts of your life. This means pushing back against bosses and careers, and realising that perhaps even some patients might DIE because you haven't given up your evenings and weekends, but you can't save everyone.

If you work for a charity you can't do everything, you can't save every starving child, there will always be more... so, harsh though it sounds, harsh though it IS, you have to look after your physical and mental wellbeing in order to function better (and for more years) in your vocational role. You can do more good in the end by looking after yourself first.

When to take this path

Having said all this stuff against vocations, it can still be a wonderful path. Maybe the money doesn't matter if you're producing great art or saving people's lives, or (as in the case of teachers) influencing people's future lives for the better.

So if you think you might have a vocation, it's definitely worth exploring it. In a later path we'll come to how you might search for your vocation, your Ikigai, your reason for living, if you have no idea what it is. But implicit in the idea of vocations is that people KNOW what theirs is, often from a young age. "I always wanted to be a tennis player" or "I always knew I was destined for politics".

To explore your potential vocation I would repeat the advice from above:

- Find out what it's REALLY like by doing some work experience early on – how does it feel? Does it make you happy?

- Find out what it's REALLY like by talking to people who have been doing it for a long time. Explore the pros and cons and think about it carefully.

But above all, don't feel bad if you don't have one. That might just be the best thing that's happened to you, because now you have CHOICE!

You can do more
good in the end
by looking after
yourself first.

Path 5
Niche

You only need to
know 5% more
than everyone else
to be expert

This path to a happy and fulfilled life is to learn about something that you are interested in, to the point where you are the expert, and you are the one who people come to, so you have security, you can perhaps charge quite a bit for your knowledge, and you can pick and choose interesting work.

For example, a friend of mine is an engineer and has made a career out of being THE guy when it comes to submarine air-conditioning systems. Which are apparently more interesting that you would expect, once you get into them.

Other niche careers could be a doctor who is specialist on treating allergies by changing diets, or a trainer who is the go-to person for courses on Agile project management, or a speaker who talks about how his experience of flying fighter jets also applies to leaders in any company – or someone who knows how to measure the real effectiveness of advertising. It could be anything that you find yourself doing, and if it interests you (that's the key part) to drill deeper and deeper into it.

You only need to know 5% more than everyone else to be expert, and that's easier than you might think, especially if you pick something very specialised.

And with the internet and globalisation it's possible to reach that 0.01% who want your service, wherever they are in the world, and although they are a tiny percentage there can be quite a lot of them – certainly enough of them who will pay a decent price for your rare knowledge.

Potential snags

One snag is that it takes a while to build up your niche knowledge, so it's not an instant solution.

And because of this time to build it up you may need to start reasonably soon. You could probably still spend your 20's messing around, but by your 30s or 40s you really do need to be homing in on your niche.

Yes, one can always specialise, and you might be lucky enough to get a niche in your 50s, but it may require your formative years to be spent on the building blocks – for example now, at my age and level of knowledge in some areas and not in others, there is no way on earth that I could learn to repair synthesisers. I would have to have spent my youth playing around

with them, modifying them, taking them apart, learning about electronics and all the different models and types, etc.

Another snag is that by the time you have the knowledge it might be out of date. Or you might happily ride the wave for a few years and then one day your one little niche gets blown away by something else.

So many niches have gone – camera film, CDs, almost every computer language and piece of hardware, maps, video shops, travel agents, many shops, newspapers, (particularly print ads), lightbulbs, big fat TVs, valves in circuits, phone booths, phone books, carburettors, petrol and diesel car engines, installing solar panels, even cash.

Then there's the difficulty of gaining and keeping the knowledge. Suppose your niche was repairing old synths and music keyboards – there are SO many to know about! And more appearing all the time!

And then, if you do have a niche, and you're deeply in it, what if you want to get out? What if you get bored or for some reason don't want to continue doing it, what else can you do? A niche is a commitment.

Tips to maximise the success of this path

My first tip is that Business to Business is always better than Business to Consumer. So if your niche can be B to B, something that companies will buy from you, then that's much better than B to C where you're selling to the public. Musicians find it hard to sell what they do to the public for a decent amount, and so do poets, and so do many photographers for everything except weddings; but if you can take photographs for *companies*, if you're the expert on badly-lit foundry photography, or fast-moving machinery, or making food look attractive, then you could be onto a winner!

But if there's something you are interested in and you seem to have a natural aptitude for it, you may as well try specialising a little bit, and see where it takes you.

Ask yourself: Could it take you into a B to B niche? Or a large or lucrative B to C niche, for example, maybe rich people's houses or cars or boats need security or decorations or music systems or other features?

See if you get more demand or less, while remembering that you are probably going down a funnel. As you go deeper, keep a close look at whether there is still enough demand, and whether the extra value you have outweighs the smaller audience.

Also keep surveying the political economic social and technical landscape for threats that would wipe out your specialist area.

I'd like to say "Keep one foot in the funnel and one foot out", or a foot in two different funnels for safely, but I don't think that's possible, I think you have to commit.

However, worst case, if your niche is wiped out, there might be something similar that you can re-learn. You'll find something else, you've already proved that you have the brain to do it once, you can do it again.

But just remember it's not secure, so save up some money, and perhaps even have a back up plan just in case.

If you take a
fun hobby and make
it into a job, you
might kill the joy

People who this path might suit

If you have an obscure thing that you like, then consider it for a way to make a living. Manga comics, beetles, making kaleidoscopes, helping people choose the right gearing for their bicycle, drawing mazes, it could be anything, in fact the odder the better! Could you earn a living from it, if you had access to the whole world as customers?

A final word of warning – if you take a fun hobby and make it into a job, you might kill the joy. My friends who have been successful from niches didn't have submarine air conditioning or hip implant geometry as a hobby, while the musicians who have tried to make it into a living have struggled, and in some cases they additionally don't enjoy music any more.

So it's good to ask yourself "Would this be sullied by HAVING to do it, having pressure to sell it, and having to take every customer, even the boring ones, and having to repeat this work every day? Churning out 100 identical pottery hedgehogs a week: will that still bring me joy?

Maybe it will, maybe it won't, but that's the question for you to ponder.

Path 6
Multi-harvest

This oddly-named path is about spreading your sources of income and your sources of happiness, so that you can be more secure, and also probably harvest more in total.

Imagine if instead of living off just the almost inedible leaves of a eucalyptus tree that nobody else can eat – a niche – you could live off a bit of everything: leaves, berries, worms, flowers, fruit, nuts eggs and ham, then you wouldn't care if one of the above was scarce for a bit.

So maybe we could be omnivores with a number of income streams, and get our happiness from lots of things in our lives rather than letting it all depend on one thing?

Pros and cons

Would it be difficult to set up a number of different income streams, or to juggle several jobs?

Would we be committed to none of them, and end up being a master of none?

Would it be less satisfying than to have a niche where we can be the best, maybe even a world expert?

I don't think so.

I think in a rapidly changing world you don't want to be dependent on any one customer or way of earning money. Also if you already have several ways then to add a new one is easy, so it makes it easier to move into new areas as soon as they come along – you are more adaptable than if you've built one great big edifice on one place. You never know which one is going to grow and which ones will fall by the wayside, so keep lots of irons burning. And don't be lazy when one goes really well and let the others all go out, but keep them all going, maybe even adding a few more.....

It's the same with happiness – it's not just the risk of losing it, but I'm pretty sure there's more happiness to be gained from dabbling in lots of things than there is from being great at one thing.

For example, if you dedicated all of your free tine to being great at tennis, so you could beat all your friends easily, would that make you happy? Who would you play tennis with? There's no point in just beating

There's more happiness to be gained from dabbling in lots of things than there is from being great at one thing

your friends, and anyway they won't be around long for that. So you'll only end up playing against the top people at your club, so it'll still be a 50/50 win outcome, but more competitive and with people you don't really like. Was it really worth it? You still haven't mastered tennis either – because you're under more pressure to get the ball right into the corner you're probably still missing the same proportion of shots as you did before you became great.

On the other hand you could have fun playing the sax badly, or well enough to get away with it, perhaps in a band in a pub; you could write some poems you never show anyone else, still play a bit of tennis just for fun when the sun is out, and you could spend time with your friends instead of all that practising on the tennis court - and instead of the tennis lessons you could learn Spanish, or photography – I'd suggest that this will add up to lots more happiness.

Genuine variety

Having a number of customers doesn't make you a dabbler – it would be better to have several completely different businesses, because this gives you much more security.

Another example – if you earned your living being Bob Dylan's sax player it would be quite likely you could suddenly lose your source of income, if Bob went off the sax, or off you – or died! (May the great man live for ever). So you could diversify and play several things for Bob, or you could play the sax for several people. But better still would be to keep bees and sell the honey as well as playing the sax for Bob, and also be an expert on repairing 3 litre Ford Capris. THAT's variety.

So I've been running training courses on a number of subjects, for a number of customers – and that does make me more secure (and also happier since I don't get bored) but that doesn't make me a true dabbler/ harvester. Even making videos is too training-related. So variety of any kind is probably a good idea, but if I was a true multi-harvester I'd be doing one or two other totally different things as well. (I'm available to play the sax for Bob, if he's reading this).

Tips to maximise the success of this path

- Start with several ways to make money – maybe a job and at least one side hustle.

- See which side hustles work.

- Maybe be self employed, or only part time employed, so you can have several of your own ideas running.

- Keep branching out, like animals evolving, to see what works.

- Don't just concentrate on the best one but keep all the viable ones going.

- Sometimes things take a while to bloom, or the environment changes, so don't kill them off unless they are costing you.

And the same with your spare time activities – be a dabbler. Don't try to compete with other people and be the best, don't try to master anything and be perfect, just enjoy the process – enjoy being in the sun and hitting the ball, enjoy the good shots, enjoy laughing at the accidents that work, enjoy the process. And enjoy making a joyful noise on your saxophone!

And a final thought about this spare time dabbling – we're not just talking about fooling around and achieving nothing. You can have a number of projects on the go, maybe you're writing a book, and writing and practising songs to play with your band in the pub, and you're learning how to code so you can make an app – these might bring happiness, maybe even money, certainly a sense of achievement, and they're all running along in parallel. You're not trying to be famous, or the best, just to harvest what you can from lots of different fields.

Sometimes things
take a while to bloom,
so don't kill them
off unless they are
costing you

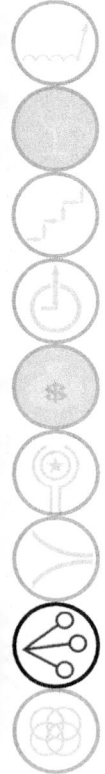

People who this path might suit

If you don't have one thing that you're great at, or you can't
see anything that has potential, or even imagine being great at
something, then that's OK, and this path will be a great one for you.
If you don't feel you have a talent, or if you can't choose one thing
above the others, then keep them all!

Path 7

The Search For Your Ikigai

The seventh and final option – not necessarily the best one, but certainly an interesting one – is to search for your Ikigai, your reason for living.

Your ikigai is the intersection of four things

- What you enjoy doing

- What you are good at

- What makes a difference to the world

- What you can earn a living doing

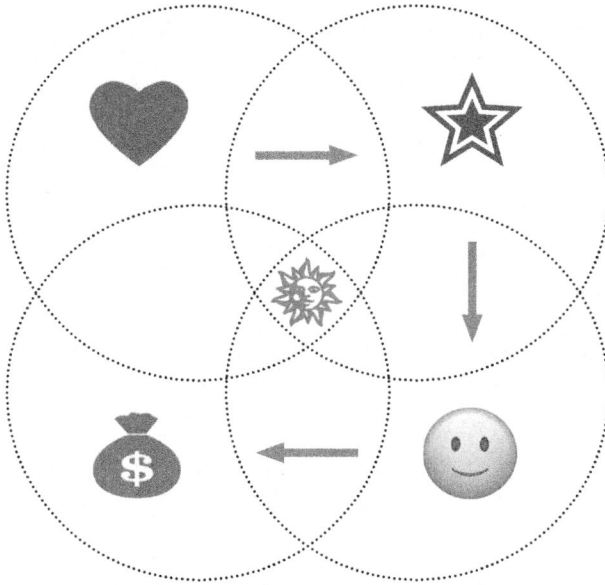

The key is to start with what you love, and then pick the parts of that which you are also good at, and then think about whether which of those make the world better.

The money comes last. If you start with "What can I make money doing?" the chances are you won't enjoy it or you won't be very good at it. Also the money must never come before helping other people because you can't prosper without first helping other people to prosper. A plan based on making money out of people without really helping them is dishonest and built on sand, so it won't last.

It sounds simple, "just follow those four steps" – but it's not.

Finding my Ikigai took me 40 years!

To find out what you REALLY enjoy doing, and what you are genuinely good at, takes a certain amount of experimenting.

My initial plan of being an engineer failed on all four circles! I didn't find it fun as I'd expected (I thought I would be designing a whole new helicopter every few weeks!), I wasn't as good at it as the others (too much detail!), it didn't feel as if it was making much of a difference to anyone, ... and the money wasn't great. Some of my friends are loving being Engineers by the way, that was just MY personal experience.

	Love	Good at.	Make a diff.	Well paid
Engineer	✗	✗	✗	✗
Manager	✗	★	✗	$
University Lecturer	♥	★	☺	✗
Freelance Trainer	♥	★	✗	$
Online videos	♥	★	☺	$

I was a better manager, and the money was better, but I didn't enjoy the things I had to do, and it was hard to make a difference. Lecturing was more fun, and you were really changing lives, though the money was a problem. Training was nearly the full set - it's fun to do, and I seem to be good at it, and it's pretty well paid. I just had a slight feeling of being on an endless hamster wheel, a drop in the ocean, as you drive around the country training another 12 people every day.

It's only been the making of videos that has really reached a big audience and I think really can make a difference to a lot of people; and I really enjoy making them too.

So it's been a long and random journey finding video-making as my Ikigai, and of course that probably wouldn't be yours. Being filmed isn't everybody's idea of fun!

Pros and cons

You can take a lot of time searching for your ikigai, and perhaps never find it.

It's a nice idea to think that everyone has a life purpose, if they can somehow find it. But nobody can prove that, and it could be that some of us are not going to be great at anything, or perhaps more likely that many of us are pretty good at lots of things – we don't have one thing that is Our Purpose. A bit like saying "There is one love of your life somewhere in the world, and you've got to find them" versus "There are lots of people, probably thousands, who you could happily spend your life with, and your life will be different - but fine - depending on which one you randomly meet at a party at college".

So maybe we should talk about finding 'A' life purpose rather than 'THE' life purpose? And while I can't guarantee it, I think it's pretty likely that you can find *something* that you're good at, good enough that people will want you to do it for them, and therefore you'll probably enjoy doing it and probably be able to earn a living from doing it.

Tips to maximise the success of this path

So the search for an Ikigai is a good idea, and could start with "What are you good at?"

But you may not know what you're good at!

- You may be modest. Perhaps your design skills or your influencing skills or your organisation skills come naturally to you and seem obvious, but others think they're really good. You could ask other people what you're good at – and *believe them!*

- You may not have discovered it yet. Charlie Mingus failed at the trumpet and the drums before he discovered the bass and become one of the best jazz bassists of all time. I had no idea that management training even existed, and making training videos DIDN'T exist, when I was working as an Engineer in the 1980s. YOUR thing is probably out there, but you might not have tried it yet. So try everything you might be good at, just to find out.

- It might take a while to become good. When I first was filmed, in a studio in LA, I found it really difficult – in fact they had to stick happy faces around the camera to make me feel I was talking to a supportive audience, and they gave me a pen to hold because my hands were going all over the place, even then we had to do lots of takes. After each one they said "That was great Chris, but can we do it one time, slightly differently…". Now I do it easily first take every time, because it's a learnable skill like anything else. We watch footballers or musicians and think "I wish I had that talent" when actually those people practice for hours every day, in order to make it look easy. So if you think you MIGHT be potentially good at something, persist for a while before deciding that you aren't!

- It might take work, to find it in the first place, and then to get to be able to do it for your living. Just because it's what you were born to do, you still have to learn how to do it. The search takes discipline to keep looking and trying things, and then, once you think you've found it, you have to learn it and then either get a job doing it or set up a self-employed way of doing it. The world may not welcome you doing it. Maybe nobody has done it before. Or there may be lots of other people also wanting to do it, so you may have to work hard on self-marketing. But it's still worth the struggle, to get all those four circles filled.

Keep searching, keep experimenting, and keep thinking!

Pitfalls and how to avoid them / make them less likely

What could go wrong?

Searching your whole life and still not finding your Ikigai? I think that's unlikely.

More likely could be settling for something you're OK at, and quite like doing, and can earn a little bit of money from, and thinking that's your

The money
comes last

Ikigai. You could develop a comfortable niche, or even build a big business, because it's what you've slipped into doing and you're quite good at it – but it's not truly the love of your life, your one life purpose, the area where you could have been great rather than just good, or comfortable.

I could have settled for being a university lecturer, and I probably would have if they hadn't made me and the rest of my department redundant. I could have told myself it was a pretty good job – rewarding and fun to do, despite the internal politics, the bad management and the terrible pay. But looking back I'm really glad I didn't settle – I'm so much more free now, and getting so much more done.

So when do you settle and when do you keep looking? Well, I think you *know*. You really do have to tick all four of the ikigai boxes – if you're not earning quite a lot of money then you're not making a big enough difference to enough people, and that could be because you're *OK* but not *great* at doing it, which is not enough. And if you're doing good business but not *loving* what you do, that's not enough either.

People who this path might suit

This path will suit people who already have something they love doing, or several things they love doing, because they've already got past the first barrier of finding something they can do.

This isn't the best path if you want to make a LOT of money, but it should lead to pretty good earnings. So if low earnings are not an option for you, but high earnings are not essential, then this path is a good option to consider.

It will also suit people who have a low tolerance for doing things they don't enjoy. For example, I just can't do a job I find boring. If I'm not learning new stuff then I can't do a job for more than a few weeks, however easy or well paid it is. That's not right or wrong, you might be different, but it's how I am. I also can't keep quiet if I feel that my boss or the organisation is going in the wrong direction – to just get on with what I've been told to do is not possible for me! So my disruptive career progression as I searched for my Ikigai was almost inevitable.

Employed / Self-employed examples of the paths

	Employed	Self employed
	Minimal office job, Casual sales, Casual manual work	Poet, Musician, Casual Plumber
	Engineer getting promoted, Sales career	Builder / property developer
	Corporate ladder: management	Build and sell your own co.
	Teacher, Doctor, Engineer	Guitar teacher, Coach
	Specialist engineer, IT expert	Consultant, Specialist importer
	Two part time jobs, Generalist job	Trainer / coach, Producer / importer of art, Non exec director
	Any of the above where you are good at it and love it	Any of the above where you are good at it and love it

Guide to choosing the best path for you

Having read this far you're probably thinking that some of those paths do not appeal at all, but some of them, maybe most of them, do have their benefits, so how can you choose between them?

If there is one of the paths that you are already pretty much on, then you can just use the advice in that chapter to decide

"Is it the right path for me?"

and

"How best to follow that path".

But if your options are open, then question is how to pick the best one from the ones that look possible for you?

Some factors to consider are:

- How important is enjoyment / happiness to you?

- How important is achievement?

- How important is time for family, friends and fun?

- How important is money?

- How self-disciplined / good at time management are you?

- How important is security? Do you want to avoid risk?

- Do you have a known talent?

- To what extent do you want to keep your options open or are you able to commit early (now??) to a path?

And: which of the above are the biggest priority for you?

Can you rule any of the choices in, or out, based on these factors?

Path	1	2	3	4	5	6	7
a Enjoy?							
b Achieve?							
c Time for F							
d Income?							
e Discipline?							
f Security?							
g Talent?							
h Community?							

Note 1 – different factors will be important to different people. Focus might be easy for you, money might be important (though it REALLY isn't correlated to happiness!), or you might be very risk averse.

Note 2 – generally money and achievement are correlated, except in the case of following a vocation where there might be a large feeling of achievement but less money earned.

Note 3 – building something big has the strongest pros and cons. It's a high risk path too.

Note 4 – Time Management (personal efficiency) / Self Discipline is very important for some of the paths, e.g. building a big project, but much less important for others. Vocations don't need much time management or self-discipline because the vocation drives you anyway – the needs of the customers, and the fact that you love doing it.

Note 5 – most of life, and success, isn't about talent. Yes you need talent to become world famous: both talent AND hard work. And I think building a business is not something anyone can do, it requires a certain set of skills that are very hard to acquire if you don't have them. And some vocations require a talent in order to do them well, for example creative vocations – but then you'll probably already have that talent because that's why you're choosing it. All the other paths really can be chosen by anyone – you can learn it!

Note 6, on early commitment: Building a business and following a vocation both require starting reasonably early in life, particularly the vocation because often you need a degree or training – and then something like music is much easier if you start young. And a niche tends to be based on knowledge you started collecting early, though not necessarily. The other paths allow you to keep your options open, if you haven't focussed on anything yet.

Maybe we should talk about finding 'A' life purpose rather than 'THE' life purpose?

It might help to think about your personality or temperament first and then have a closer look at the paths that correspond to it, as follows:

Are you a quiet logical person: an "analytical".

Or are you an outgoing logical person: a "controller".

Or maybe a quiet emotional person: an "amiable"

Or an outgoing emotional person: an "enthusiast"?

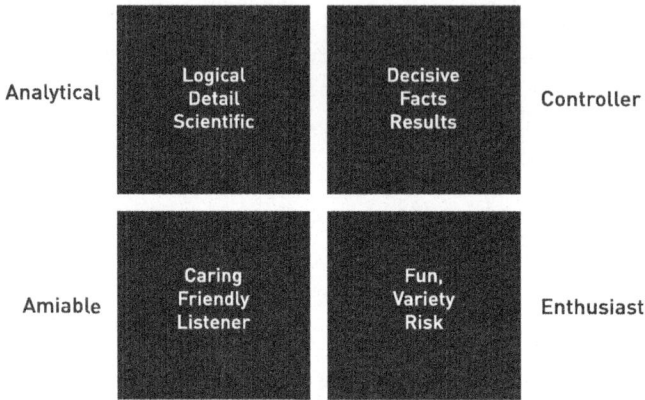

	Logical Detail Scientific	Decisive Facts Results	
Analytical			Controller
Amiable	Caring Friendly Listener	Fun, Variety Risk	Enthusiast

Sometimes these categories don't resonate for people but often they do (and your friends might have useful views on you which one you are!), and if you know which box you fit mainly into it might help you to choose the best life path, as follows:

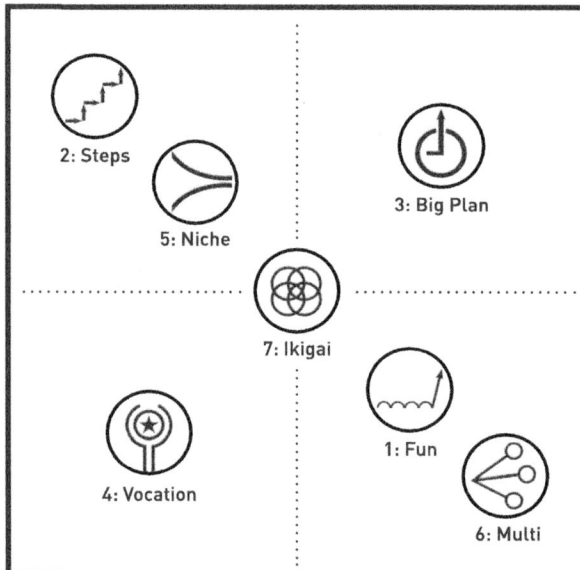

2: Steps

5: Niche

3: Big Plan

7: Ikigai

4: Vocation

1: Fun

6: Multi

The logical Analytical person would be well suited to building a career steadily with minimum risk, and then (or instead of that) perhaps focussing on a niche and becoming a specialist expert.

The decisive Controller will be the one to build their own business, or the one to go up the corporate ladder – in both cases, planning for the future, doing whatever is needed to succeed.

The fun-loving Enthusiast is most likely to go for the "fun while it lasts" option, or perhaps multi-harvesting from a variety of activities since they do love variety.

And finally the caring Amiable could well choose a vocation, particularly one where service is done, like nursing or teaching.

Here's another way to think about your ideal path: a Venn diagram:

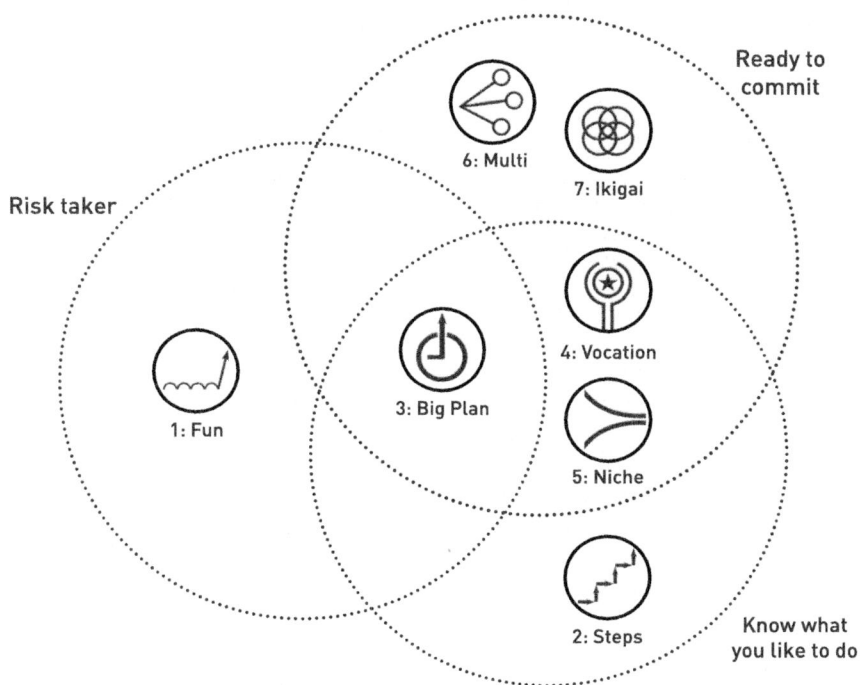

They practise for
hours every day,
in order to make
it look easy.

Diagnostic Chart

Or perhaps you would prefer a decision tree:

Which path are you travelling at the moment?
Which path would you ideally travel?
This chart might help you to think about these questions.

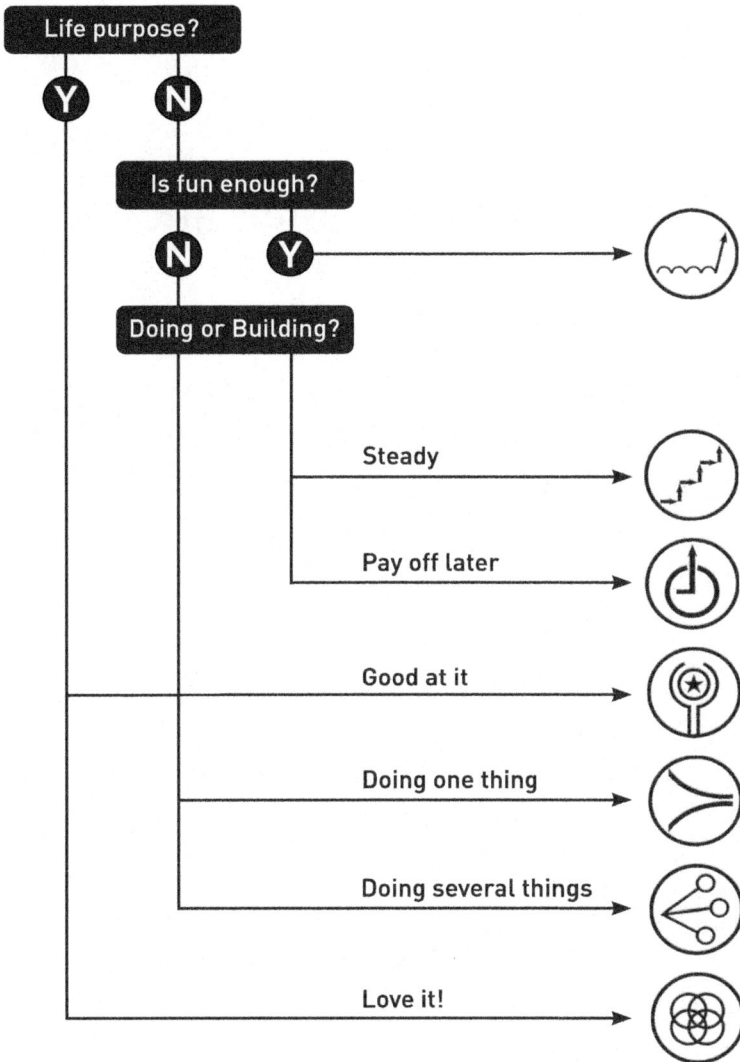

Combinations of paths

Some of these 7 paths are not really compatible – you have to choose one or another. But some can be combined, or you can take one for a while and then change to another. So they can be done in parallel or in series.

For example, "Fun Until It Runs Out" is a good starting path and can be followed by a Niche, or Looking for your Ikigai. And your niche could BE your Ikigai. Your vocation could also be your ikigai, but may not be.

So let's explore the combinations in a more scientific and thorough way:

Taking one path, then another

1: Fun

Could be followed by:

   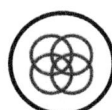

2: Steps   5: Niche   6: Multi   7: Ikigai

2: Steps

Could be followed by:

3: Big Plan   5: Niche   6: Multi

3: Big Plan

Completion of your big plan
could be followed by a new phase

   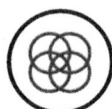

3: Big Plan   5: Niche   6: Multi   7: Ikigai

4: Vocation

Could be followed by refining it:

5: Niche

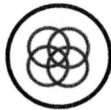
7: Ikigai

5: Niche

Could be followed by evolving it:

2: Steps

3: Big Plan

6: Multi

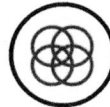
7: Ikigai

6: Multi

Could be followed by homing in:

3: Big Plan

4: Vocation

5: Niche

7: Ikigai

Could be followed by working on it in different ways

3: Big Plan

4: Vocation

5: Niche

6: Multi

Examples of the above

Fun for a few years could be followed by almost anything, though it might be a bit late to train for some vocations (e.g. doctor) and might be a bit late to build a big plan (also I don't think a Big Plan type of person is likely to take a decade off!).

Building in steps could end up as a Big Plan, or homing in on a niche, or several niches (less risk – you can see which ones works out best).

Big plan could be followed by homing in on one particular area - or a bit of a life crisis where you wonder why success and money hasn't made you happy!

Vocation followed by niche: "I'm going to home in on one part of what I do and become a real specialist in that".

Vocation followed by Ikigai: "I thought this vocation would make me feel fulfilled but it hasn't. So what else is there I could do instead....?"

Niche followed by big plan would be: "this niche has potential, and I can't supply it all, I'm going to employ people and build up a company".

Multi-harvesting followed by niche: "this one area is the one I like best, I'm going to home in on just this part".

Ikigai could be followed by one big thing you're going to do, or that you've realised what your vocation is, or you have realised that there's a niche you can really be great at, or you have found several things and you'll try them all and see which one works out best.

Travelling a combination of two paths at once

The lines in the next diagram indicate paths that can be combined – for example you could pursue some types of vocation while having fun. e.g. poetry or music, (but probably not medicine!) or you could be discovering your niche or looking for your Ikigai during your fun path. And your vocation could involve building something big, e.g. a school in Africa (paths 3 & 4 at once). Or your big project could be done in small safe steps: 2 and 3.

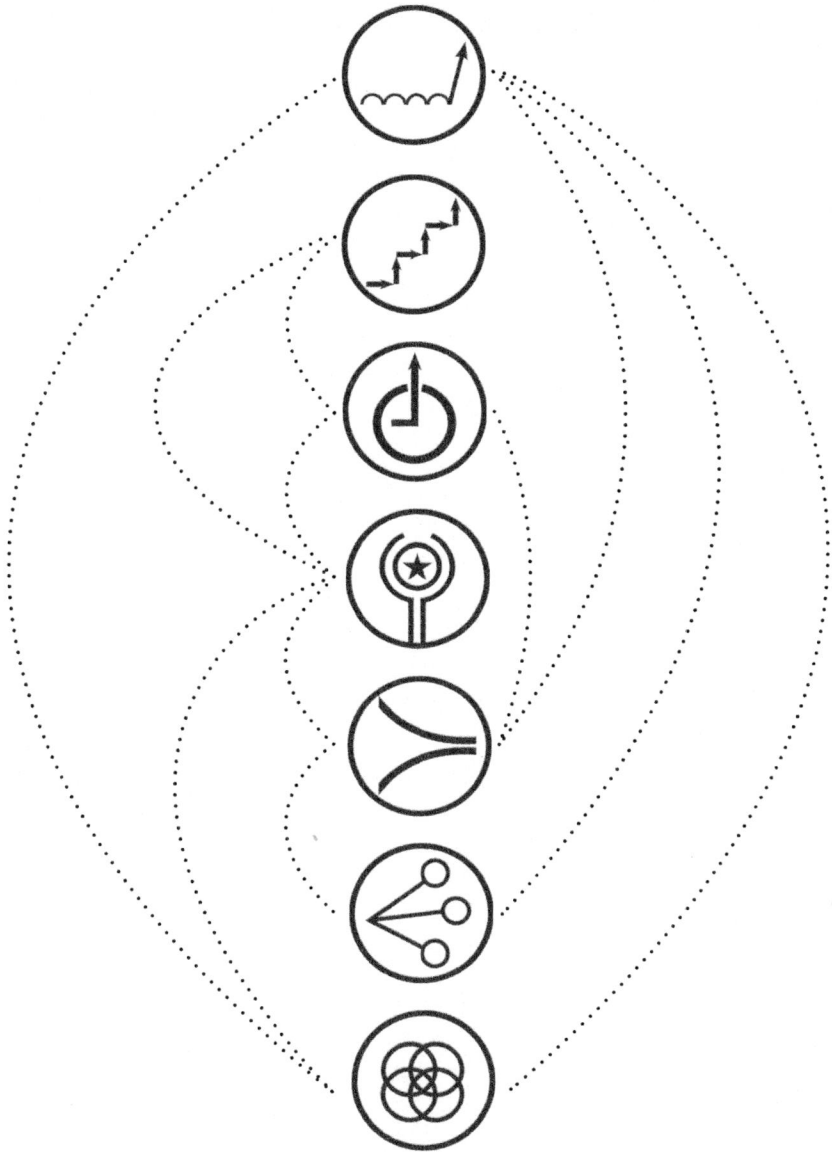

More combinations could be for example 2 & 4: building your vocation one step at a time (e.g. building up a charity) or 4 & 7: realising that your ikigai is the same as your vocation (it easily could be) or your niche could be similar, adaptable to fit your ikigai.

And if you have several niches that would be a combination of 5 and 6. Also you could discover and develop a number of sources of income while taking your fun path – that would be 1 + 6.

Your niche could be occupied and built up, at the same time: 5 and 3.

In fact most paths could be combined, though I think some are incompatible, for example combining 3 and 6: multi-harvesting while also building up your one big plan.

Just because it's
what you were born
to do, you still have to
learn how to do it

Some Final Questions

Which paths struck a chord with you?

Here are some questions to ponder about whichever path(s) you are thinking of taking:

Path 1

- Could you live with fun but without achievement?
- If you are currently taking path one, are you spending a bit of time thinking about future objectives, and future things that you could achieve?

Path 1A

- Are you wasting your time at work?

Path two

- Do you have something you're working towards?
- What would you do after you reach that?
- Are you enjoying the climbing process?

Path three

- Are all your eggs in one basket and if so, how risky is that plan? What is the percentage chance of it succeeding?

Some paths can
be combined, or you
can take one for a while
and then change to
another

- And what would you do after you have succeeded?
- Are you enjoying the process?
- How much are you having to give up at the moment?
- Are you caught in the sunk cost fallacy? (where you can't quit your path because you've invested so much time into it up to this point)
- Could you delegate more?
- Do you have a backup plan?

Path 3a

- Are you driven by money or principles/love?

Path four

- Are you sure it's your vocation and not an inherited or assumed role?
- Is your vocation fun and well paid enough to keep it for your whole life?
- What would you do if you weren't doing your vocation?
- What are you having to give up because of the time you have to spend on your vocation?
- Do you have an undiscovered vocation?
- If you *had* to have one, what would your vocation be?

Path five

- Could your niche disappear if something changes in the market or the world?

- What's your backup plan?
- Could you niche to be widened?
- Could/ should your niche be narrowed even more?
- What's the most fun or best paid part of your current niche?

Path six

- Could you add more variety to the ways you earn a living?
- Could you start a(nother) side hustle?
        ...or at least investigate the viability of one?
- Are there any strands you should ditch? Because they're not fun or not well-paid enough?

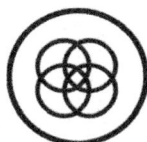

Path seven

- What do you love but are not good at, ...and could you get better at it?
- What do you love and you're good at but are not earning a living from?
- What can you do that the world <u>really</u> wants?
- Are you "settling"?
- Ask your friends to answer the above about you.
- What would you love to do if you had the talent for it?
- What talents <u>do</u> you have which you're not monetising or fully exploring?

Disclaimers

This book isn't perfect! There could be other paths which I haven't identified, and pitfalls within a path that I haven't spotted.

But I hope it's food for thought, and helpful. Many people never stand back and think about where their lives are headed – they are busy enough surviving, or keeping their job, or doing well at their job. Or they have settled for their life even though they aren't particularly happy, or they could be happier, or more successful, if they took a different path. Sometimes people assume that they can't have a better life than the one they are in. Pass it to your friends if you think they need to read it!

Schools don't help, and there don't seem to be any models or structures to the question of careers. Normally it's assumed that you should get the best paid job you can, or the one with the best (financial) prospects, and then everything else will follow. But we know that's not a great plan, for anyone really.

So if this book can help you to stand back and think more clearly about your life options, that's great.

If you disagree with it, or want to add to it, feel free to contact me via my website, chriscroft.com, or via LinkedIn. I'm always interested in new ideas ...

Printed in Great Britain
by Amazon